THE KIDS BOOK OF POOP

By Professor Poopy McDooDoo

THIS BOOK BELONGS TO SUPER POOPER:

____

All inquiries about this book can be sent to the author at ProfessorPoopyMcDooDoo@gmail.com
Published in the United States
ISBN: 978-1-7359665-3-3
Paperback

My name is Professor Poopy McDooDoo.

Today I am going to teach you everything you need to know about poop.

First, the most important thing to know:
EVERYBODY POOPS!!

Babies poop a lot.

Grandmas. Grandpas. Aunts.

Uncles. Cousins. They all poop.

And not just your family. Teachers poop.

Policemen poop.

Firefighters poop.

Athletes poop.

Rock stars poop.

Actors poop.

Even the president poops.

Some important facts you
should know about poop.

Poop comes in lots of colors. Brown is best.

Poop comes in lots of shapes and sizes.
Small.
Medium.
Large.

Extra-large.
Pellet-sized.
Long and runny.

What's the best size for a poop?

A couple of inches is just right.

Did you know that everything
you eat turns into poop?

Bacon and eggs for breakfast . . . turn into poop.

A burger and fries at lunch . . . more poop.

Even a nice healthy dinner . . . ends up as . . . poop.

Poop can be some pretty stinky stuff.

Sometimes, lots of poop means lots of toilet paper. Too much can be a problem.

BUT THE MAGIC POOP ERASER WORKS EVERY TIME!

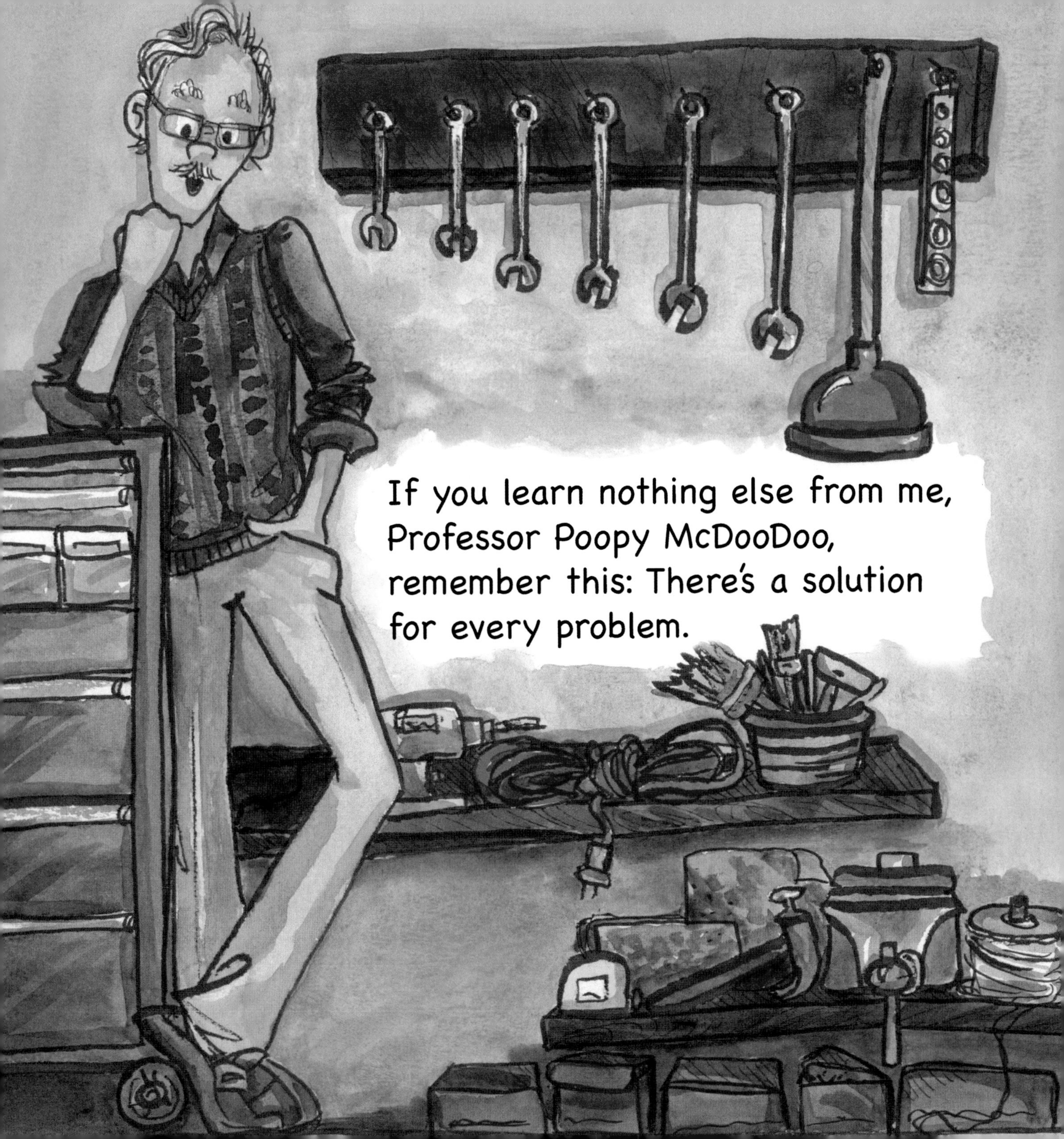
If you learn nothing else from me, Professor Poopy McDooDoo, remember this: There's a solution for every problem.

When it comes to pooping, there are some important things you should know.

Pooping doesn't stop you from doing other things. While you poop . . .

You can read.

You can paint.

You can talk.

You can sleep.

You can draw pictures of your poops.
You can even name your poops.

T-Rex
Runt
Little Bit
Hercules
Weiner Ball
Daisy
Tiny Dancer

Poop is a great topic for jokes. Here's a good one.

When you poop, do you wipe with your left hand or your right hand?

ANSWER: I don't use my hands, I use toilet paper!

There you have it. Everyone poops. No need to ever be embarrassed, even if you have to poop at school.

Now please excuse me . . .
I have to go poop!
Diploma of Poop

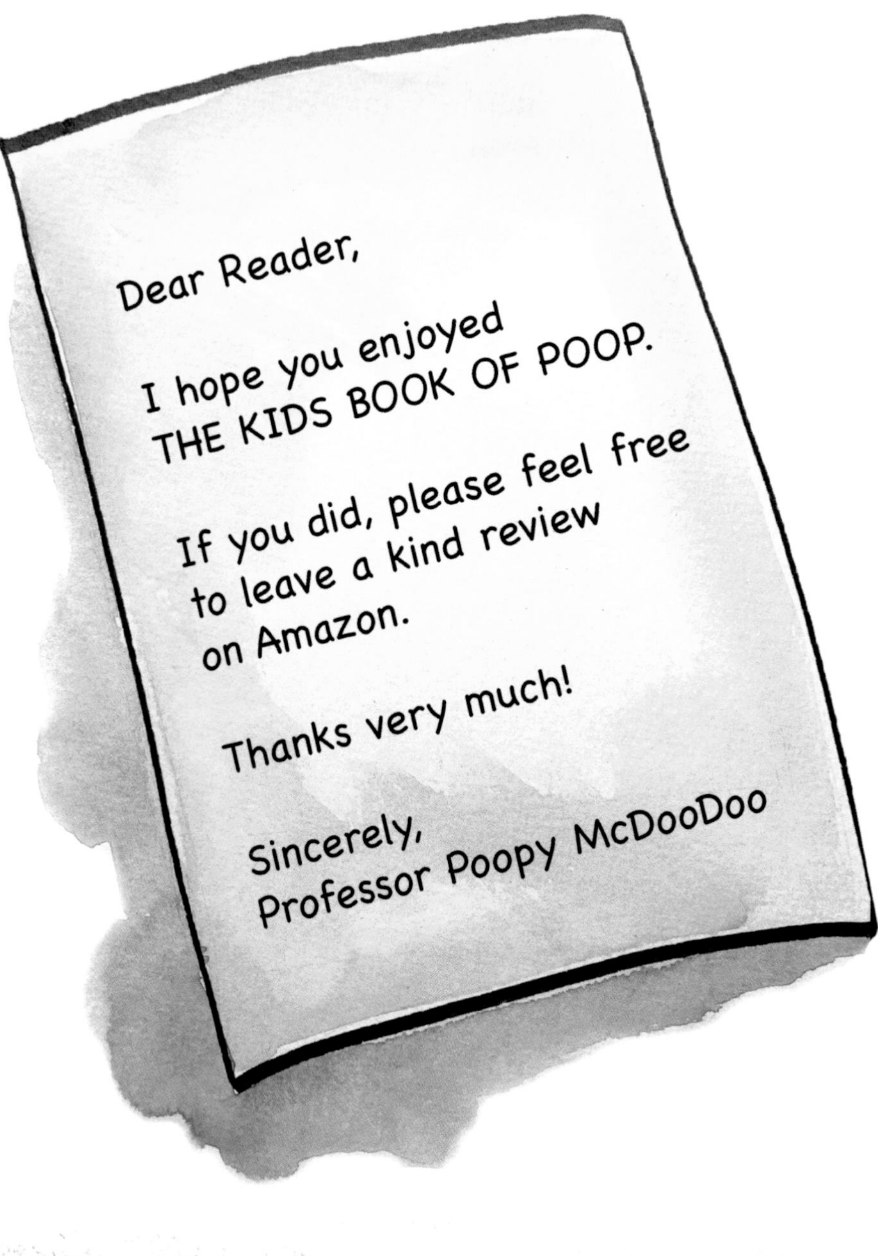
Dear Reader,
I hope you enjoyed
THE KIDS BOOK OF POOP.
If you did, please feel free
to leave a kind review
on Amazon.
Thanks very much!
Sincerely,
Professor Poopy McDooDoo

Made in the USA
Middletown, DE
24 February 2021